Daily Life in
THE
PILGRIM
COLONY
1636

PAUL ERICKSON

Clarion Books • New York

Clarion Books
a Houghton Mifflin Company imprint
215 Park Avenue South, New York, NY 10003
Copyright © 2001 by Breslich & Foss Ltd

The text was set in Berkeley Book.

www.houghtonmifflinbooks.com

Printed in Hong Kong

Library of Congress Cataloging-in-Publication Data

Erickson, Paul, 1976–
Daily life in the Pilgrim colony 1636 / Paul Erickson.
p. cm.
ISBN 0-618-05846-X   PA ISBN 0-395-98841-1

1. Pilgrims (New Plymouth Colony)—Juvenile literature. 2. Pilgrims (New Plymouth Colony)—
Social life and customs—Juvenile literature. 3. Massachusetts—History—New Plymouth, 1620–1691—
Juvenile literature. 4. Massachusetts—Social life and customs—To 1775—Juvenile literature.
[1. Pilgrims (New Plymouth Colony) 2. Massachusetts—Social life and customs—To 1775.]
I. Title: Pilgrim colony 1636. II. Title.

F68.E75   2001
974.4'8202–21
2001017203

10 9 8 7 6 5 4 3 2 1

Conceived and produced by Breslich & Foss Ltd, London
Series Editor: Laura Wilson
Art Director: Nigel Osborne
Design: Phil Richardson
Photography: Miki Slingsby

CONTENTS

THE WORLD OF THE PILGRIMS

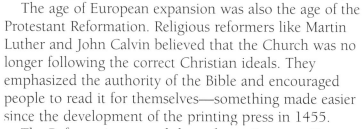

I n 1620 a band of English people crossed the North Atlantic to establish a small colony in what is now called New England. The story of these Pilgrim Fathers has become an important part of the history of the United States. At the time, however, the colony was simply part of the spread of European culture and influence. For more than a century, the nations of Western Europe had been establishing colonies and trading posts around the world, aided by improvements in navigation such as the compass and by the development of guns and other powerful new weapons.

The age of European expansion was also the age of the Protestant Reformation. Religious reformers like Martin Luther and John Calvin believed that the Church was no longer following the correct Christian ideals. They emphasized the authority of the Bible and encouraged people to read it for themselves—something made easier since the development of the printing press in 1455.

The Reformation spread throughout Germany, France, Switzerland, the Scandinavian countries, Holland, and also England. During the Tudor period (1485–1603), the Catholic Church in England broke away from Rome, and eventually England became a Protestant country under Elizabeth I. There were some people, however, called Puritans, who felt that reforms in the Church of England were not going far enough. Beginning in the 1580s, the more extreme Puritan groups separated from the Church of England and began holding their own religious services. The government did not like these Separatists. They were fined, imprisoned, and banished from England. Some were even executed. The Separatists held their church services in secret or fled to other countries, where they formed communities with fellow believers.

Meanwhile, the idea of the New World had excited all levels of English society, whatever their religion. The Spaniards had brought back fortunes in gold and silver from their territories in Mexico and South America, and the English were eager to start making money from the lands that England had claimed in North America, where fish and furs were to be found in abundance. The drawback to this enterprise was the huge expense. Maintaining a colony in the New World might cost as much as £15,000 ($22,500) per year. At a time when a person could live on £20 ($30) per year, this was a great deal of money.

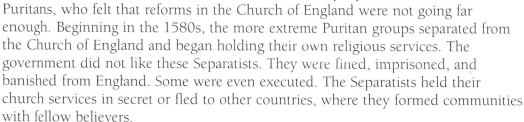

Joint-Stock Companies

To pay for these expeditions, people created joint-stock companies, which are like modern corporations that sell their shares on the stock market. People who bought shares in the joint-stock companies would receive a share of any profits made by the company. An example of one of these was the Virginia Company, which established the first lasting English settlement in the New World, at Jamestown, Virginia, in 1607.

The Pilgrims

In 1607–08 a small group of Separatists fled England for Holland, where their religious ideas were accepted. They became known as Pilgrims. But although they were free to worship as they wished, they did not feel at home. Being English subjects, they found it hard to find work, and they feared that their children would lose touch with English traditions. They looked to the lands that England claimed in the New World in the hope that they could live there as English men and women while retaining their Puritan religion. During 1617–20 they reached an agreement with a group of London adventurers (investors) to back their efforts to establish a colony in the New World. A joint-stock company was formed, with the adventurers putting up most of the money. Shares in the company were given to the future colonists, who were supposed to pay off the price of their trip and earn their shares by working entirely for the company. In return, the company promised to send over food and supplies. The company also obtained a patent, or license, from the king that authorized them to settle on land in the New World.

In September 1620, the company set out on two ships, the *Mayflower* and the *Speedwell*. The *Speedwell* was forced to turn back for repairs, so its passengers joined those on the *Mayflower,* which continued the voyage alone. In November the weary company sighted land, and after exploring, they found a good place to settle. On December 21 they disembarked at their new home, which they named New Plymouth, after the port they had sailed from in England.

Left: Mayflower II, *a full-scale reproduction of the type of early-seventeenth-century merchant ship that carried the Pilgrims to America. It is a small ship by today's standards: 106 ½ feet long, with a beam of 25 ½ feet and a draft of 13 feet.*

THE NEW WORLD

I n the seventeenth century, published accounts of the New World spoke of a wonderful place with huge areas of land that had never been farmed, exotic plants and animals, oceans full of fish, and precious metals. The Pilgrims believed that they would soon make good profits in their new home.

Although the land of North America was untouched by the plow, it was not untouched by human beings. Until a few years before the Pilgrims arrived, Native Americans of the Patuxet tribe had lived in the area surrounding the site of Plymouth. In addition to hunting and fishing, the Patuxet planted fields of corn, beans, tobacco, and squash. They cleared the land by setting fires, which also removed the undergrowth from the surrounding forest, making it better suited for hunting. However, in 1616–17 the Patuxet and other local tribes were stricken by smallpox and other diseases. Most likely, European traders who had entered the region brought with them these Old World diseases, to which the Native Americans had no natural immunity. In some places, up to 90 percent of the population died. The Patuxet were entirely destroyed, so that when the Pilgrims arrived, they found only empty villages strewn with bones. The sole survivor, Squanto, had just escaped from captivity in Europe, where he had been taken before the epidemics struck. Homeless and tribeless, he came to live with the Plymouth settlers, whom he taught to grow corn and catch eels during their difficult first winter. The settlers thought that the epidemics and the assistance of the local Indians showed that God favored their colony. The tribes that survived disease were so weakened that they decided to make friends with the invaders rather than attempt to fight them. The chief of the Wampanoag tribe, Massasoit, signed a peace treaty with the Plymouth settlers in the fall of 1621.

Despite agreements like these, the native tribes and the new settlers did not really understand one another. The Indians never really grasped the colonists' ideas about owning land until they found themselves shut out of most of their former territory, while the colonists never regarded them as members of their community. From the start, the settlers were unable to seriously consider the idea that they, as "civilized" people, could become friends with the Indians, whom they thought of as "savages." This lack of trust, together with growing tension over land and terms of trade, would lead to war between colonists and Indians in the 1670s.

Right: *This map dates from around 1635 and is from an engraving by Willem Janszoom Blau, a Dutchman. Although the eastern coastline of North America is rather inaccurate, it does show how much of the New World had been charted by Europeans.*

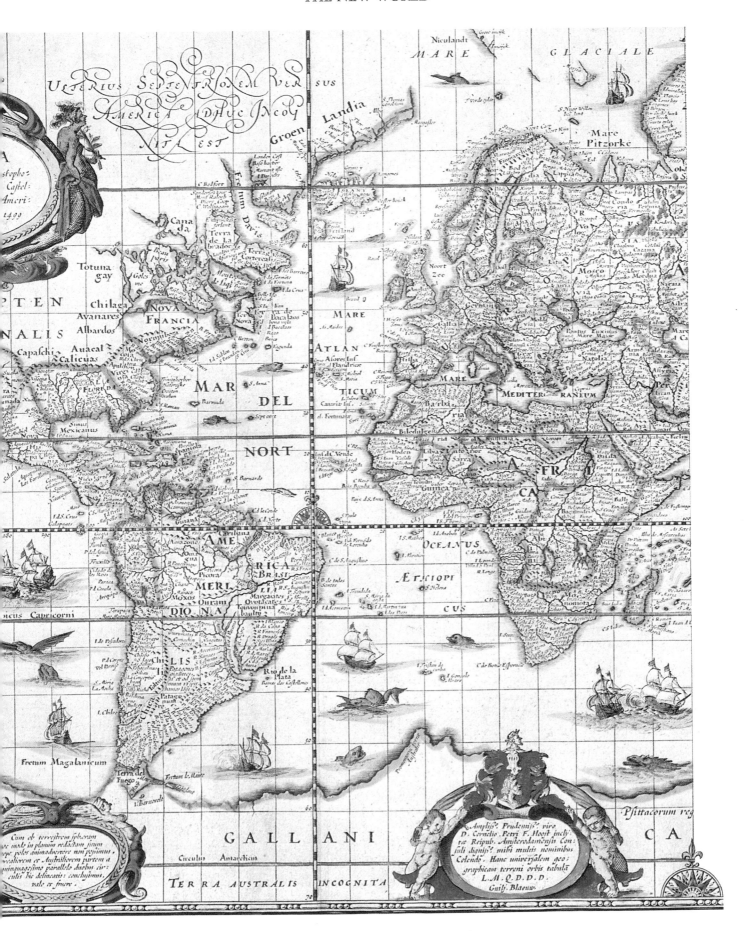

BUILDING A NEW SOCIETY

When the Pilgrims arrived on the *Mayflower*, the first things they needed were food and shelter. But before the crops could be planted and the huts built, they had to come to an agreement about how their new society was going to work. Of the 102 *Mayflower* passengers, fewer than half were "saints"—that is, members of the separatist Puritan church. The rest, known as "strangers," were ordinary people. There were many choices to be made about how they wanted to worship, be governed, and make a living before they could form a proper community. As time passed, the proportion of saints became even smaller as more settlers arrived who were strangers.

By 1630 the Pilgrim colony was no longer the only one in New England. In 1623 a Puritan minister named John White had organized the Dorchester Company with the goal of starting another colony. In the next few years, this would grow into the large Massachusetts Bay Company. In 1630 a fleet of eleven ships sent out by the company arrived in Salem, bearing more than 700 colonists. During the next decade, thousands more would come to this colony.

Despite differences in their background, both the saints and the strangers were expected to attend the separatist church services. Different religious ideas were not allowed, and people who followed other religions were forced to leave the colony. Few complained, however, because although many were not saints themselves, they thought the Puritans' ideas were good.

Plymouth was not a democracy in the modern sense. The first written constitution was called the Mayflower Compact. It was drawn up just before the Pilgrims landed in 1620. The men who signed it agreed to obey an elected governor. Women and male servants were not allowed to sign. There was no book of laws until 1636, and no "bill of rights" until 1672. Basically, the governor could do what he wanted, unless it was against the laws of England.

As time passed and the colony grew larger, a more complicated system of government offices and laws was developed. The only people allowed to vote were "freemen." Apart from the exclusion of all servants and women, there were no rules to say who could or could not be freemen, but usually they were over thirty, well thought of, and comparatively wealthy.

Above: *When the Pilgrims arrived, they made dugouts and wigwams* (right) *for shelter while they built their permanent houses.*

Left: *In their wooden travel chests, the settlers packed their more fragile and precious possessions: glassware and pewterware for use at the table, carpets to lay on tables and beds, and the family Bible.*

Below: *For many years, metal items like this Norfolk latch were not made in Plymouth Colony; instead, they had to be imported from England or acquired from the larger Massachusetts Bay Colony.*

"We . . . having undertaken . . . a voyage to plant the first colony in the Northern parts of Virginia . . . do solemnly and mutually, in the presence of God and of one another, convenant and combine ourselves together into a civil body politic, for our better ordering and preservation."
Mayflower Compact

Left and above: *The settlers copied the wigwam design from the Native Americans and used local materials.*

NEW PLYMOUTH: TOWN AND COLONY

For the first ten years, the colony of New Plymouth consisted of one settlement: the town of Plymouth. The Pilgrims chose this site shortly after their arrival in 1620 because it was near the now abandoned farm fields of the Patuxet Indians and because a stream of fresh water flowed nearby. By January 1621 the Pilgrims had built an assembly hall and had laid out plans for storehouses and homes.

Defense against Indian attack was considered when the Pilgrims designed the town. In early 1621 they moved cannon from the *Mayflower* to the top of a steep hill above the town. In 1622, fearing attack by the Naragansett Indians, they built a palisade (strong fence) around the town's edge. This palisade was built of dressed logs (logs with the bark and branches stripped off). Inside the fence was enough room for the dozen or so families of the town to have houses and small garden plots. In the same year, they also began building a fort at the top of the hill where they had earlier placed their cannon, but this was not finished until the following spring. This fort also became the Pilgrims' place of worship.

After a while, the settlers' fear of Indian attack was overcome by their desire for more farmland. In 1627 the colonists bought the London adventurers' shares in the settlement. Cattle and land that had belonged to everyone were divided up among the men who took part in the buyout. Many of the great lots of land lay far from the town of Plymouth. To the north, toward the Jones River, and to the south, toward the Eel River, the land was good for farming and grazing cattle.

This bird's-eye view of Plymouth in 1636 (*right*) shows a landscape still largely wooded but gradually giving way to fields and pastures. The land around the town center is thickly populated, but the surrounding countryside is broken only by the occasional farmstead or tiny village. Roads and trails cut across the landscape at intervals, following the line of old Indian paths. At least one runs from Plymouth up toward Boston in the Massachusetts Bay Colony, and farmers regularly make the overland trek to sell their cattle or crops at the markets there. Gradually the Pilgrims are transforming this land into what they have called it: a new England.

Above: *The fort and palisade were built from the plentiful local timber.*

Right: *As soon as they could, the settlers built houses and gardens like the ones that they had known before they set out on their voyage.*

THE FAMILY

The year is 1636. Jonathan Prentiss, thirty-six years old, is the owner of a farm not more than a mile from the town of Plymouth. Born the youngest son of a farmer back in England, he came to the colony in 1621 on the ship *Fortune*. He knew that he could not expect to inherit land from his father, so he wanted to move to a place where there was plenty of land to be had. During his first years in the colony, he lived and worked in the household of a family inside the town of Plymouth. He also traded for beaver pelts with the Indians. In 1625 he even accompanied Governor William Bradford on a trip to buy a trading post in Maine.

In 1626 Jonathan married, and a year later, in the buyout of 1627, he was granted some cattle and forty acres of land in the Eel River valley. By 1636 he is, by Plymouth standards, well off, with property worth over £100 ($150). In spite of his success, he is always looking for more things to do. At the moment he is trying to buy some more land, and he has gotten involved with the colonial government by advising the courts on how to set wages and prices.

Rebecca Prentiss is thirty-seven years old. She came to the colony from London in the fall of 1625 with her first husband, who had hoped to set himself up quickly with a large house and lots of land. Unfortunately, he died in the winter of that year, leaving Rebecca in an unfinished house with two children to care for. It was at this time that she met Jonathan, who was especially kind and helpful to her during that terrible winter. They were married the following spring.

Although she has remarried, Rebecca still has the rights to the small plot of land near town that she and her first husband were given when they arrived, as well as the possessions her husband brought from England. The land has been leased to another family, and Rebecca pays taxes out of what she makes in rent.

The children from Rebecca's first marriage are Sarah, now age sixteen, and Isaac, age twelve. Since her remarriage, Rebecca has had another son, Thomas, who is seven, and an infant girl named Anne.

Edward Jeffrey comes from a family that lives inside the walls of Plymouth. He is twenty years old and unmarried, and he doesn't yet own any land himself. Three years ago, his father made an agreement with Jonathan Prentiss for Edward to live with the Prentiss family for five years, so that that he could learn husbandry (farming). Such arrangements are very common throughout the colony, for it is the surest way to teach a young man a trade. Jonathan benefits too, because he needs the extra labor for his farm.

Edward Jeffrey lives with the Prentiss family. He hopes to start his own farm when he finishes his apprenticeship.

*The Prentiss family stands together in a rare
moment of inactivity. The two elder children, Sarah and
Isaac, have kept their father's name of Winstead and will
inherit the land given to him on his arrival in the colony. At
the moment, however, they are happy with their new family
and are very fond of Thomas and baby Anne.*

THE HOMESTEAD

The Prentisses live not far outside Plymouth, in the Eel River valley. Close by the river are marshes, broken by groups of trees, and meadows where cattle graze. Farther from the water is the woodland where Jonathan Prentiss has cleared more fields. It is here that he built his house in 1632. Like most families in the colony, the Prentisses are farmers, growing almost everything they need from their land. The cultivated fields produce grain to feed the family, with enough left over to be traded to Boston in exchange for manufactured goods from England. They keep cows, pigs, sheep, and poultry to provide them with milk, meat, wool, and eggs. The center of domestic activity is the farmyard that surrounds the house. The area is enclosed by a fence made of wooden stakes. At night the milk cows are kept in here in the cowshed. In the morning they are milked in the dairy house that is attached to the shed before being released to graze in the meadows.

Above: *The cutting and shaping of lumber is done by hand. The adz (top) is used to square the cut timber into beams, and a drawknife (bottom) is used to smooth rough surfaces.*

Reeds gathered on the banks of coastal inlets and streams are used to make thatched roofs in the traditional English style (left). But thatch burns very easily, and after a number of fires, a law was passed in 1627 forbidding its use. Since that time, most houses have been built with shingle roofs (far left).

One Francis Eaton, carpenter, did serve me in the building of my house before his untimely death. This early time has not been without hardship, for trouble and disease come often to our midst.

Jonathan Prentiss

Rebecca Prentiss's Garden

On the front and side of the house is the garden. Here Rebecca grows vegetables—cabbages, turnips, leeks, parsnips, onions, carrots, and radishes—for the family to eat. There are no potatoes or tomatoes. New Englanders have only just heard of these, and Rebecca does not want them in her garden.

She also grows herbs such as dill, rosemary, Saint John's wort, and valerian, both for kitchen and medicinal use. Although most of the plants here are kept because they are practical, Rebecca has also planted a small bed of daffodils, roses, and other pretty flowers around the doorway. She is happy that they brighten up the washed-out grays and browns of the muddy farmyard.

Storage

The largest building on Jonathan's property is the barn, which holds the grain and hay after the harvest. The pigs are kept in sturdily built pens to stop them from escaping and eating the crops. In order to provide extra storage, small sheds with low sloping ceilings, called lean-tos, are placed against the house, barn, and fence. Pitchforks, buckets, barrels, hoes, and other tools are kept inside.

INSIDE THE HOUSE

The house consists of a large open room or hall, which is separated from a smaller storage room or buttery by an immense fireplace and chimney. In the buttery the overhead planks can be removed so that Jonathan can store tools and lumber easily and Rebecca can hang nets of onions and cured meat from the rafters, where they can stay cool.

The interior walls are made of whitewashed plaster applied over a lathe of sticks (*below*). Behind the sticks lie the straw and dried moss that help to keep heat inside the house in winter. The floor is made of sawed wooden planks. By English standards this is a luxury, for in the Old World, where timber is becoming scarce, most house floors are of earth or stone. Otherwise, the Prentiss house is very simple. A few solid pieces of furniture and a rug draped on the table (protected by a sheet at mealtime) show that the Prentisses are quite well off, but the local authorities do not like people to have fancy decorations.

The hall is where everything happens during the day and where everyone sleeps at night. As well as a large table, it contains heavy iron cooking pots, earthenware and pewter dishes for the table, tools taken in for repair, a gun and bandolier, books—including the family Bible—and a cradle. There is also a large brick hearth where all the cooking is done. Rebecca spends much of her day here, moving among the cooking pots, which need her constant attention.

There is no running water, so it must be fetched from the spring in buckets. If hot water is needed, it is heated in a big cauldron over the fire. The house is heated by the central fireplace and chimney. Though large, they do not provide much warmth, and the house is cold and drafty in winter. Although there are many trees, the Pilgrims do not build snug log houses in the way that later settlers will. They continue to use the construction methods and styles that they knew in England.

Lighting the house is an even greater problem than heating it. The waxed-paper windows (*above*) are small to prevent heat from escaping and the

Right: *Folded-up mattresses are kept in the corners of the main room. The children pull them onto the floor to sleep on at night. Their parents share a real bed with the privacy of curtains (see diagram of house plan).*

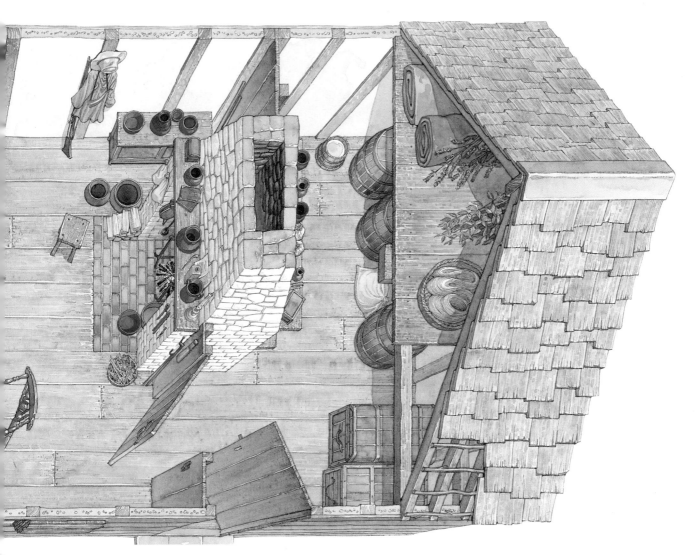

soot-blackened interior does not reflect much light. Oil lamps, often called rushlights, are used at night, but even during the day the interior of the house is dark and shadowy.

The pitch of the roof is very steep, originally to help water drain from the thatch. The rough boards on the walls are unpainted and have become gray from the weather. The windows are simply small openings in the walls. They are covered with waxed paper, because glass is not yet made in New England and imported glass costs too much. Real windows, with small diamond-shaped sheets of glass set in lead frames, are so valuable that when people move, they take them to their new house along with the furniture.

The Prentiss home can boast a few fancy touches. The door has iron hinges and a latch that Jonathan picked up from a blacksmith in Boston. Until several years ago, these were still made of wood, like everything else in the house.

EARLY MORNING

T he sun is just coming up on this crisp fall morning. As the light grows, chickens in the yard begin to stir. A rooster crows. Soon the family will be up too. The fire has burned down low during the night, and Rebecca's first task is to pile on more sticks and a new log from the woodpile in the corner.

Breakfast is usually something simple, just

enough to keep everyone going until dinner is served in the middle of the day. This morning, it is cornmeal porridge ("hasty pudding") with some imported raisins added as a special treat. The food is served on wooden boards, or trenchers, and the family eats it with wooden spoons.

The meal is over quickly. Usually Jonathan is out the door as soon as he has finished eating, off to work in the fields with his sons and Edward. But today he is dressed in his best, ready to set out for Plymouth town to attend a special meeting of the General Court. Edward is in charge of the harvest today, and he soon goes off with Isaac and Thomas at his side. Not long afterward, Jonathan also leaves and begins his walk north along the road that will bring him to town. Rebecca, Sarah, and little Anne are left behind. Rebecca and Sarah will clear off the table, wash the dishes, and begin the daily work of the household. It will not be long before baby Anne is given a few chores to do.

Center: *Cooking takes place on the wide brick hearth. Pots can be covered with embers to cook the food inside them (above). The griddle (lower right) has legs so that it can be placed over a bed of coals.*

Chores Before Breakfast

Rebecca gives Sarah a nudge and sends her out to get a bucket of water from the spring (*below left*). The spring is far from the house, and when Sarah gets back, her mother is already preparing breakfast. She sets the heavy wooden water bucket down on the hearth and decides to wake her brothers.

But Isaac and Thomas are already getting dressed, having sensed that breakfast is not far off. As Rebecca likes to say, "They're just like the young piglets in the yard, so quick on their feet when they hear you coming with the slop bucket!" The boys also have chores to do before breakfast, grinding up some more fodder to feed to the farmyard animals and clearing away the mattresses and blankets that litter the floor. Edward does the heavier work, bringing in more wood from the woodshed (*above*) to feed the fire. Then they all wash their hands and faces in a bowl and sit down at the table for the first meal of the day.

Left: *The Prentisses are now used to drinking spring water. In much of Europe, people—including older children—mainly drink beer for fear of catching diseases from polluted rivers and wells.*

GETTING DRESSED

I n England, laws govern what a person can wear. Luxurious clothes are reserved for important and wealthy people. Plymouth Colony does not have such laws, but opinion is strongly against people dressing "above their station." Both men and women usually have two outfits, one for daily use and the other for Sundays and special occasions. The difference between them is in the quality and color of the fabrics used. Shirts and coifs (women's headware) are made of white lockram, a type of linen fabric. Everyday clothes are usually woolen or linsey-woolsey, a coarse cloth made from wool and linen. They are brown or russet, which are easy colors to create dyes for. Jonathan bought his best outfit in Boston not long ago, a plum-colored suit of drugget (a fine wool fabric) with brass buttons. He also bought a new dress for his wife, of sad green buckram (linen). The word *sad* here means dark. The Pilgrims of Plymouth often wear sad colors like dark green and black, which are regarded as solemn and suitable for church.

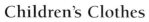

Children's Clothes

Sarah and Isaac, and now even Thomas, dress very much like their parents, except that they go barefoot in warmer weather. Until this year, however, Thomas dressed the way that little children in Plymouth dress. Before the age of seven, boys and girls go about in simple shifts with ties at the shoulders. When necessary, parents can grab hold of these to keep their children from running off and getting into trouble.

Above and right: *Men and women sleep in their long cotton shirts. In the morning they put on long woolen stockings held up by garters tied just above the knee. Jonathan then puts on his breeches (trousers that run to just below the knee) and a doublet (jacket) over his shirt.*

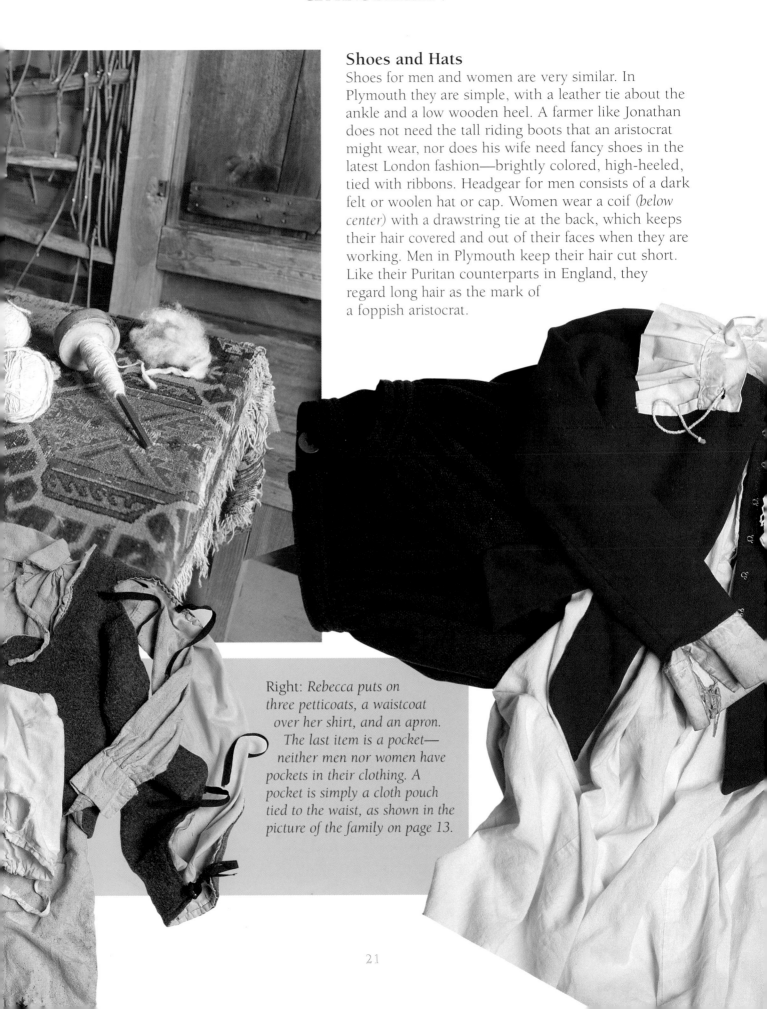

Shoes and Hats

Shoes for men and women are very similar. In Plymouth they are simple, with a leather tie about the ankle and a low wooden heel. A farmer like Jonathan does not need the tall riding boots that an aristocrat might wear, nor does his wife need fancy shoes in the latest London fashion—brightly colored, high-heeled, tied with ribbons. Headgear for men consists of a dark felt or woolen hat or cap. Women wear a coif (*below center*) with a drawstring tie at the back, which keeps their hair covered and out of their faces when they are working. Men in Plymouth keep their hair cut short. Like their Puritan counterparts in England, they regard long hair as the mark of a foppish aristocrat.

Right: *Rebecca puts on three petticoats, a waistcoat over her shirt, and an apron. The last item is a pocket— neither men nor women have pockets in their clothing. A pocket is simply a cloth pouch tied to the waist, as shown in the picture of the family on page 13.*

MEN'S WORK

For the Plymouth farmer, the yearly cycle of planting and harvesting begins as soon as the ground thaws in March. The land is first broken with the plow and then combed over by the harrow. Crops imported from Europe, such as peas, wheat, and rye, are then sowed over the ground. Corn—a crop that the settlers adopted from the Indians—is grown in a slightly different way. Instead of sowing the seeds, the farmer buries them inside little mounds of dirt. When the corn shoots appear, he plants beans, gourds, and pumpkins (called by the settlers "pompions") in the mounds as well, following the Indian practice, in order to keep down weeds. But while the settlers plant Indian-style, unlike the Indians they do not take constant care of their fields. During the summer, apart from some weeding and hoeing in May and June, they usually leave the crops to fend for themselves. Scarecrows and fluttering bits of cloth on long strings keep away the more timid birds, but beyond that, the task of protecting the growing crops against birds and stray animals is usually given to the younger children.

Above and left: *Colonists brought with them a variety of tools for use in farming.*

Right: *Work in the fields is hot and exhausting. A hat helps prevent sunstroke and a container of water is a welcome companion for the midmorning break.*

> *I have heard that any man who shall kill a wolf shall be granted five bushels of corn, for they beset our flocks and we have much trouble to be rid of them.*
>
> Edward Jeffrey

Summer to Winter

In July and August, the farmers cut winter hay for their livestock from the meadows, which are common land belonging to everyone. They move slowly across the fields, swinging their long-handled scythes to cut the grass. The cuttings are left on the ground for several days in order to "cure" in the sunlight. Then they are gathered up and stored on the hayracks in the barn. An acre of meadow is expected to produce a ton of hay.

In late August and early September, the farmers take in their field crops—peas, rye, and wheat. October is the time for the Indian corn, gourds, and pumpkins. During the winter, the corn is husked and the kernels are separated from the cobs. Wheat and rye are threshed and winnowed to separate out the seeds. These activities keep the men busy until the next round of planting the following spring.

WOMEN'S WORK

While the world of her husband extends from house to field to faraway trading posts, the world of Rebecca Prentiss and her daughters is centered on the house, garden, and barnyard.

Every morning and evening, the cows must be milked. As soon as breakfast is over, Sarah leads the cows into the dairy house, where she sits on a low stool and milks them over a bucket. Then she feeds them some cornmeal and lets them out into the pasture.

Keeping the house clean takes a great deal of work, especially since there is no running water. Sarah makes frequent trips out to the spring to fill the bucket, while her mother scrubs the wooden trenchers and utensils left over from breakfast. Waste water is simply thrown out the door. Any rubbish on the floor is swept into the fireplace with a broom made of fine twigs, and grease spots are removed from the planks with soap and water.

From time to time, Sarah removes the ashes from the fire and stores them in a dry place for use in making soap. Soap is usually made in the spring, just in time for the traditional spring cleaning. Sarah helps her mother pour water over the ashes, which have been placed in a big hopper. They collect the liquid—called lye—in a trough beneath. Rebecca then pours the lye into boiling fat, and she and Sarah take turns stirring all day until it turns to soap. They then pour the soap into large wooden containers where it will set and be stored for use throughout the year.

Fresh food must be eaten quickly or preserved in some way. Extra milk is made into butter or cheese; meat is salted or smoked; vegetables are dried or pickled. In preparation for winter, the women hang nets of onions from the rafters in the cool loft above the buttery, together with pumpkins and various other dried vegetables.

Left: *In the morning the women of the house search the garden for vegetables to put in the stew pot. Since it is fall, there are many fresh items to choose from—turnips, onions, parsnips, and pumpkins. In other seasons, there are also peas, and wild strawberries, blueberries, raspberries, and blackberries.*

Left and below: The women are responsible for looking after the farmyard animals. When the hogs are slaughtered in November, Rebecca and Sarah are very busy making bacon, hams, and sausage to last the whole year. Sarah not only milks the cows but churns the cream to make butter nearly every day. Rebecca uses the wool from the sheep to make some of the clothes needed by her family.

Laundry

Bedding and clothes have to be kept fresh as well. Because beds are made from either straw or feathers (if you are lucky!), their contents get musty very easily. Every day, Sarah helps her mother hang the bed blankets and mattresses outside on fences and bushes, so that they can air out.

Washing clothes is a tedious but relatively infrequent task, since people usually wear the same clothes every day. Jackets and suits can go for several years without washing, but linens and undergarments, as well as little Anne's clothes, require more frequent attention. To do laundry, Rebecca and Sarah build a large fire in the yard to heat a cauldron of water. The clothes are then boiled in the cauldron to break up grease, while Sarah stirs them with a wooden stick. They are then rinsed and hung out to dry on a convenient bush or fence.

TRADE AND DEFENSE

From the very beginning, the colonists have intended to pay off their debts to the people who backed them and then make money by trading with England. It is no surprise that even now, in 1636, trade in natural resources such as fish and fur and corn is closely regulated and protected by the colonial authorities.

The Plymouth colonists have been clever in selecting good sites for trading posts. In 1627 they built a post on Long Island Sound, for trade with the newly established Dutch colony of New Amsterdam (today's New York); in 1630 they obtained a patent for trading rights on the Kennebec River in Maine; and in 1633 they set up a trading post by the Connecticut River, on a piece of land they bought from the local Indians. However, most people in the colony are not allowed to trade in fur. The profits are reserved for the "undertakers," those few colonists who were in charge of paying back the London adventurers after 1627. Some of the more ambitious among the undertakers have tried to use their position to build personal trading empires, but their schemes have never really panned out.

By 1636 the importance of large-scale fur trade in the daily life of the colony is declining. The trading post by the Connecticut River was abandoned in 1635. The new city of Boston, in the rapidly growing Massachusetts Bay Colony, is replacing Europe as the destination for Plymouth's goods. Farmers regularly make the overland trek north, following ancient Indian trails, or sail small boats along the coast. In Boston, they find good prices for their cattle and grain, and the city's merchants have access to European imports, which they sell to the farmers in return.

Left: *Beaver fur is popular in Europe and can be bought from the Indians in exchange for metal goods, beads, and alcohol.*

Left: Long before the Pilgrims established their settlement, English ships fished the local waters. The Pilgrims have brought plenty of fishing tackle in the hope of developing a trade in fish, but they are never really successful, since their boats are often wrecked or their catch stolen by pirates.

When I am of age to fight, I shall join with my father and Edward in the ranks and carry a musket, but I have not yet the strength to master such a weapon.

Isaac Winstead

The Militia

In addition to the danger from the local Indians, there is the possibility of the colony being attacked by the Dutch, the Spanish, or the French. Although these countries are not at war with each other, their rulers have little control over fights that break out so far from home. The Pilgrims organized a militia in Plymouth soon after they landed, and now each town has its own. Every man between the ages of sixteen and sixty has to train, and every household must keep a gun. The militias drill regularly under the command of the town captains. They practice walking in formation and firing volleys.

Above and right: A Matchlock musket and several pikes. Soldiers stand close together, keeping the ends of their pikes pointing outward like the quills of a porcupine.

MAKING AND MENDING

I f something is broken on the farm, or if Jonathan needs a new bucket or a new shed, he will attempt to do the task himself or else he will turn to his neighbors. There are many skilled craftsmen in Plymouth, but they do not practice their trade on a full-time basis—like everyone in the colony, they spend most of their time farming. Nevertheless, they are happy to help out a neighbor in return for some corn or bacon, or for a promise of work at a later date.

Many of the day-to-day items for the house and yard are made and maintained by the family. Jonathan enjoys woodworking, and he keeps his home equipped with stools, tables, beds, bowls, and platters. Anything made of pottery, metal, or glass comes from either England or the Massachusetts Bay Colony. These items are hard to repair, because in 1636 there is no blacksmith or potter in Plymouth.

Bricks for building chimneys and hearths are not made in Plymouth either. There is a brick-maker in Salem, however, who has been in business since 1629. On the other hand, Plymouth does have a gristmill for grinding corn to make cornmeal. The charge is fixed by colony law at a pottle of corn for each bushel ground. Jonathan finds it very convenient to take his harvest there for grinding in the fall.

Above: *The coastal marshes are full of reeds that the colonists use for making baskets and thatching the roofs of their houses.*

Right: *Barrels are necessary for trade. Everything is shipped inside them, from butter and molasses to fur and salt fish. This barrel shows the barrelmaker's tools.*

Preparing Wood

There is plenty of timber for carpentry and coopering (barrel-making) in the colony, but it must be carefully selected and cured (dried) before it can be used. Lumbering is done in the winter, when there is less undergrowth in the forest and no farm work. The logs are either dragged to the saw pit (*below*) by teams of oxen to be sawed into planks, or they are split to make shingles, clapboards, or barrel staves. Since all of this work is done by hand, it takes a very long time!

Left: *Turning sheep fleece into clothing is a long and intricate process. First the fleece must be carded, or combed, to clean the wool and straighten the fibers. Then a spindle is used to twist the wool fibers into thread, getting it ready for the next process of dyeing and weaving.*

Below: *The saw pit allows two men to saw a big log laid across the pit. One handles the top end of the saw* (right) *while his partner works the other end from below.*

Clothing

Rebecca makes and mends clothes for the family. There is no professional weaver in Plymouth, so Rebecca must have her husband buy cloth, thread, and needles in Boston. Clothing is never thrown away. If an item gets too ragged to wear, it is set aside so that the cloth can be used to patch other clothes. Quilts and bedcovers are also made from old clothes, and many families are kept warm at night by material from their grandparents' old worn-out clothing.

COOKING AND EATING

Once the remains of the morning's hasty pudding have been cleared from the table, Rebecca begins work on the main meal of the day, dinner, which is typically served between 11:00 A.M. and 12:00 noon. Today's dish will be a salt-fish-and-vegetable stew—"bubble and squeak," as it is often called—served with more hasty pudding and bread. One reason why cooking takes so much time is that there are no grocery stores in the colony. Products such as bread, butter, and cheese must be made at home. The most common bread, called "rye and Injun," is made with a mixture of cornmeal, rye, and barley flour. Baking is done once a week and takes an entire day. On these days, as soon as they wake up, Sarah and Rebecca build a fire in the brick-and-clay oven in the barnyard. When the oven is hot enough, they scrape the embers out of the oven quickly and place the dough inside to bake in the heat held by the bricks. Butter and cheese are made with milk from the cows in the farmyard. It is Sarah's job to beat the fresh creamy milk in a churn until the fat separates from the buttermilk. Then she collects the fat and presses it into pats of butter. Cheese-making is a still more complicated process, requiring a press to drain fluid from the cheese, and rennet—an acidic substance from the stomach of a young cow—to curdle the milk.

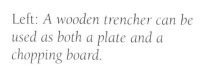

Top left: *A colander used for separating curds from buttermilk.*

Near left: *Indian corn gives higher yields than wheat and rye and is quickly replacing them.*

Left: *A wooden trencher can be used as both a plate and a chopping board.*

Right: *Mussels are plentiful, although regarded as poor fare.*

Food from the Sea

The New World provides an abundance of food for the skillful fisherman. In the spring, the coastal streams and rivers teem with alewives (a type of fish) and eels, which are caught in great numbers for use in stews and pies. In the fall, most families living on the coast also go after offshore fish, such as cod and herring. Cod is a very popular food back in Europe. In fact, the king of Spain is said to favor New England cod for his Good Friday meal. The fish is prepared for storage by salting and drying—"making fish," as the process is called.

Less popular but more accessible are shellfish and lobsters, which can be picked up in the tidepools and shallows along the seashore. In 1622 a visitor to the colony wrote of the lobsters with particular enthusiasm, claiming that they were "so large, so full of meat, and so plentiful . . . as no man will believe that hath not seen." However, not everyone is quite so enthusiastic about lobster, and laws have been passed so that servants do not have to eat it too often.

Left: *Rotating spits are used to roast whole animals over the open fire. A common task for young children is to sit on a stool at the hearth and turn the spit for hours on end.*

Below: *Iron spoons and knives are the common table utensils. Forks are rare, although the governor of the Massachusetts Bay Colony is said to have brought one with him in 1630.*

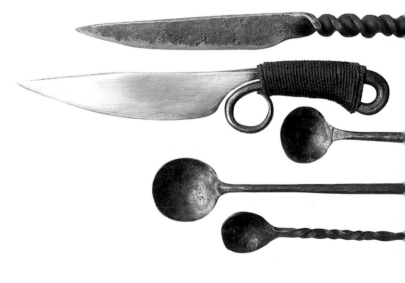

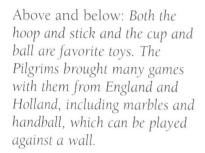

THE CHILDREN'S DAY

The Puritans who settled the New England colonies believed strongly that they should follow the teachings of the Bible, both in matters of worship and in daily life. Being able to read was, therefore, highly valued. However, in contrast to the Massachusetts Bay Colony, there are still no "common," or public, schools in Plymouth. Almost all learning takes place in the home, without the help of textbooks, so the level of a child's education depends on his or her parents.

It is hard to say how many people can actually read and write, for only ministers and lawyers need to use these skills for their work. Most families own a Bible, and most property owners can sign their names on legal documents. When he was in England, Jonathan learned to read, write, and calculate well enough to "cast accounts" of what he sells or harvests. In the evenings, he gives lessons to all his children, making them read aloud and recite verses from the Bible. Rebecca was not taught to read as a child, but she has persuaded Jonathan to give her lessons as well.

Isaac is showing signs of becoming a "scoller." He already has more learning than his father, and has become a favorite of William Brewster, an elder in the Puritan Church, and often visits him. He likes to spend time in Brewster's library, with its hundreds of books on history, philosophy, and religion, written in English, Latin, and Greek. If he were to study with Brewster for a few years, he would be ready to enter the new college to be founded at New Towne to train for a career in law or the church.

Above and below: *Both the hoop and stick and the cup and ball are favorite toys. The Pilgrims brought many games with them from England and Holland, including marbles and handball, which can be played against a wall.*

Doing the Chores

On these busy fall days, there is little time to spare. Isaac and Thomas are at work in the cornfield with Edward. It was just this past year that Thomas became old enough to work in the fields, and he is proud to be out there alongside his father and brother. At home, little Anne is too young to be of any help yet, but Sarah is very busy. As well as milking the cows, she sweeps the house and yard and grinds up fodder for the barnyard animals. She tends the fire and removes the spent ashes (*above*), and helps her mother with the cooking.

Although there are many chores to be done, the pace of life in Plymouth usually leaves young people plenty of free time. There is the countryside to explore, and for children used to the cities of Leyden or London, there are many opportunities to get lost if they wander too far from the settlement!

I love to dandle her upon my knee and hear her sweet prattle, but I would that Anne were of an age to help with the work of the house, for there is much to do.
Sarah Winstead

Above: *Anne's cradle is beside her parents' bed. The mattress is a small sack filled with straw. Every morning Rebecca takes the wet, dirty straw out and replaces it with fresh straw.*

GOVERNMENT AND RELIGION

When Jonathan arrives in Plymouth for the meeting of the General Court, the town is already buzzing with activity. Everywhere groups of men are standing about discussing what will happen. Jonathan talks to his neighbors; they are all worried that the colony's laws are not good enough, and it is for this reason that the court is about to meet for the second day in a row. Others are trying to stir up opinion against the governor and his assistants, saying that it is unfair for them to be the only people who can grant land. But before any trouble can break out, a rattle of drums announces that the governor and the magistrates are processing to the meetinghouse to begin the proceedings. The men quickly head up the hill after them.

It is the freemen of the colony, like Jonathan and his neighbors, who are permitted to vote for government officials and magistrates, to run for office, and to be heard at sessions of the General Court. Only about one third of the adult males in the colony are freemen, and they are the only ones who are allowed a say in politics. Nobody really minds this. In fact, the General Court often has trouble getting the freemen to show up for meetings and has recently had to fine some of them for failing to attend.

The General Court, meeting regularly four times a year, is the most powerful governing body in the colony. It is responsible for taxing the colonists, making laws, and hearing court cases. There is also a Court of Assistants, consisting of the governor and his advisers, which takes care of business between meetings of the General Court. The most common cases brought before the courts are disputes between people over property or rights to land. The judgments of the court are based for the most part on the traditions of English common law.

Right: *The fort meetinghouse is used for both political and religious purposes.*

The Pilgrims at Church

Every Sunday the town of Plymouth is summoned to the fort meetinghouse by a drum. A company of the militia marches up the road. The men, who are carrying muskets, are dressed in their Sunday best: dark-colored suits and tall black hats. Behind them walk the governor and preacher wearing long black robes, and the rest of the company follows. There are two services, one in the morning and the other in the afternoon, and everyone is required to attend. The Sunday dinner, which is eaten between services, is prepared the night before, to be eaten cold the next day. This is because the Pilgrims believe in keeping a strictly religious Sabbath, and anyone who works on a Sunday can be taken to court.

Like any other public meeting, the Pilgrims' church service begins with a prayer, which is read by the minister or ruling elder. Next comes a Bible reading and a sermon by the minister or the elder based on that text. The sermon is the most important part of the service. If a particularly impressive minister is visiting, people will come to town from far away to hear him speak. There will be crowds of eager onlookers, and many people will have to settle for standing room outside the door and windows. Sermons are often published in written form and are very popular.

After the sermon, a communion of bread and wine may be given if there is a minister present, and psalms are sung by the congregation.

Crime and Punishment

In 1631 John Billington, a *Mayflower* passenger, was tried, found guilty, and hanged for killing a man with whom he had quarreled. Murder is one of very few crimes that can result in execution. Most of the really serious crimes are punished by banishment from the colony. For lesser offenses, such as drunkenness or adultery, payment of a fine, a public whipping, or a public apology is ordered.

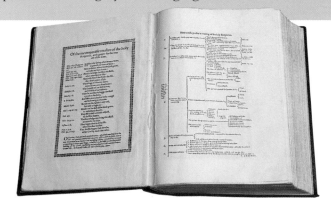

Above: The Pilgrims take the Bible very seriously. At the front of this one, there are instructions showing readers how to get the most spiritual help from their Bible study.

HEALTH AND MEDICINE

When the first Pilgrims arrived in 1620, they brought with them a large supply of "physic" (medicines) and a doctor, Samuel Fuller. In 1621 he helped the Pilgrims earn the goodwill of the local Indians by healing some who had been wounded in a fight. In 1629 Fuller was called to the Massachusetts Bay Colony to look after the dying wife of Governor John Endecott, and the next year he was sent there again, to help the citizens of Mattapan. Unfortunately, the doctor himself died of a fever just three years later.

A multitude of deadly illnesses faces the colonists, including influenza, tuberculosis, smallpox, and pneumonia. Vitamin deficiencies are also common because very few people eat fresh, uncooked fruit or vegetables.

Most doctors in the seventeenth century based their cures on the ancient Greek system of humors. They believed that the body contained four humors, or fluids: blood, phlegm, yellow bile or choler, and black bile. If people had either too much or too little of one of these in their bodies, they would become ill—to enjoy good health, the humors had to be kept in balance.

Herbal remedies (right) were made from plants such as lavender, feverfew (above left), and others (below) including camomile, fennel, and tansy.

Medicine from the Garden

If the colonists get sick, they are most likely to turn to their own gardens and kitchens for a cure. Home remedies made from commonly found herbs are often more effective than treatment from a professional doctor. The housewife's garden produces, among other things, coltsfoot (for coughs), St. John's wort (for aches), valerian (an antidepressant), and comfrey (to speed up the healing process). Medicinal herbs are ground up using a mortar and pestle. They can then be made into infusions, which are prepared with boiling water to be drunk or inhaled, or turned into a paste or ointment to put on the skin. Medicines prepared by boiling or steeping herbs in beer or wine are also popular.

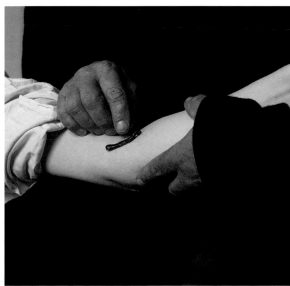

Above: *The doctor applies a leech to his patient's arm. He hopes that, in this case, the balance of the humors will be restored by removing some blood. On other occasions he may decide that he needs to administer different humors to achieve a balance. He knows the humoral properties of many substances, including different herbs and other plants, so that he can devise a suitable cure for a range of illnesses.*

Childbirth

Although all doctors at this time are men, women can find a profession in midwifery—overseeing the birth of babies. Midwives are usually older women with many children of their own. Their job is to ease the mother's pain, to help with the delivery, and to keep the mother and baby healthy after the birth. The hardest task is to keep the mother alive—at this time, one out of every five women dies in childbirth.

END OF THE DAY

T he shadows on the road are long by the time Jonathan returns from Plymouth. He and his neighbor, Robert Bartlett, round the last bend just in time to see Edward, Isaac, and Thomas coming back from the fields. While the others go inside to wash up before supper, Jonathan lingers with Robert for a moment at the garden gate. The General Court this day has created a committee to revise the laws of the young colony, and both men wonder what this will mean. But already it is dusk, and soon Robert waves good-bye and continues toward his home.

Inside, Sarah has been at work preparing some sops, broth to be eaten with bread. After supper there is another round of chores to be done. There are pots and platters to clean and livestock to feed. In addition, the children must be given their lessons and recite their prayers. Jonathan listens intently so that he can correct any mistakes they make.

At this time of autumn, the days are still long, and there is more time for leisure between sunset and bedtime. The family sits around the fire on high-backed settles that help to block drafts. Jonathan, Edward, Rebecca, and even Sarah light up long clay pipes to "drink tobacco." The family enjoys roasted apples dipped in mead or light beer, their favorite after-dinner refreshment. The fire is burning low, and the oil lamps and rushlights (*right*) give only a feeble light.

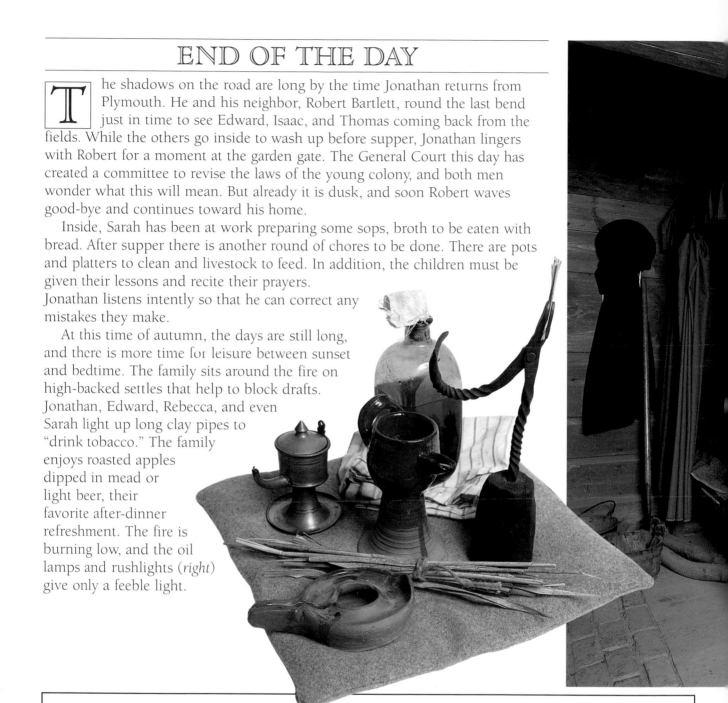

Left: *Smoking is a popular pastime for both men and women in seventeenth-century New England. Tobacco caught on quickly in Europe during the previous century, after it was introduced from the Americas by returning explorers. In Plymouth some tobacco is grown locally, but most is imported from Virginia and the Caribbean. The long clay pipe shown here is called a churchwarden pipe. The long stem can be broken off in pieces as it wears out.*

Below: *Chamber pots are necessary at night—much easier to use than making a trip outside in the dark.*

Bedtime

Before long it is time for bed. Jonathan reads a passage from the Bible and prays for the safety of his family and of the colony. The children's mattresses are moved into the middle of the floor and covered with sheets, blankets, and pillows. Edward is sent to check the shutters and the front door. Jonathan checks the gun and bandolier. He then taps out the rushlight and climbs into bed, confident that, by God's providence, he and his family have found a lasting home.

Left: *The bed curtains of the parents' bed keep out drafts and provide privacy. Mattresses are most often stuffed with hay or cornhusks, but rich people have feather beds. The mattress is held up by ropes that are attached to the frame of the bed.*

These ropes often needed to be tightened by using a bed key, hence the familiar expression "good night, sleep tight."

SPECIAL OCCASIONS AND CELEBRATIONS

There is more hustle and bustle than usual in Plymouth on Thursday morning, because it is market day and the local farmers are coming into town. Many of them bring wagons full of corn, eggs, butter, live chickens, and barrels of apple cider. Others come driving pigs, geese, and other livestock before

them. A man named John Barnes has recently set himself up as a local trader, and he always brings some imported goods from Boston to sell at the market. This week he has some casks of wine, a case of cutlery, and some silk ribbons for the ladies. Some members of the Wampanoag tribe arrive, bringing baskets and brooms made by the women. The baskets are especially popular. They are so tightly woven that water can be carried inside them!

Since there are no stores in the colony, market days are when people do their shopping. The Pilgrims brought this custom with them from England. Rebecca Prentiss is out haggling with the cobbler for a new pair of shoes. Jonathan and his friends have gone off to a nearby house where a friend is pouring them mugs of beer. The beer is very good, and the friend is thinking of opening a tavern in town if he can get permission from the magistrates. The men's talk is mostly about politics and trade, especially the cattle prices up in Boston. Through an open window they can see the town constable pacing back and forth, carrying his heavy staff and looking out for people who have had too much to drink or who are trying to sell liquor or guns to the Indians. Boys are running about playing tag, to the delight of the giggling girls and the dismay of the cackling chickens, which do their best to keep out of the way.

Right: *Jonathan and his friends drink their beer from big leather jugs and beakers made of animal horn.*

Above: *"The First Thanksgiving," a painting by Jennie Brownescombe c. 1914.*

The First Thanksgiving

The Puritans object to the many religious holidays of the Church of England, including Christmas. But if a special occasion arises, there is sure to be a celebration, such as the one that took place in the fall of 1621, when the Indian chief Massasoit and a large company of his men came to visit their new allies in Plymouth. For three days the entire settlement feasted on wild ducks, geese, and turkeys, and on the deer brought by the Indians.

Although this event will in time become known as the first Thanksgiving, the Pilgrims saw it as a traditional autumn harvest festival. A proper Puritan thanksgiving is a day of fasting and prayer intended to give thanks to God for some particular event or accomplishment. The first thanksgiving of this kind in the Plymouth Colony was declared by Governor Bradford in 1623, when prayers for rain during a dry spell were finally answered.

Our harvest being gotten in . . . many of the Indians coming amongst us . . . whom for three days we entertained and feasted; and they went out and killed five deer, which they brought to the Plantation and bestowed upon our governor. Edward Winslow, a later governor of Plymouth Colony, writing about the 1621 harvest.

Plymouth Succotash

This dish could be made in bulk for winter eating and kept frozen outside. Chunks were broken off and thawed as they were needed. It has traditionally been associated with Plymouth and with Forefathers' Day.

1 quart pea beans	1 medium turnip
6 quarts hulled corn	5 lbs. fowl
6 lbs. salt beef	

Soak the beans overnight, then cook and mash. Boil beef and fowl until tender and save broth. Cut up the turnip and cook in the broth. Cut the beef and fowl into 1½-inch cubes. Combine all the ingredients and let boil together for about an hour. Stir frequently to prevent sticking. Let cool, always uncovered, and stir to prevent souring. Serve in bowls.

THE PILGRIMS' PLACE IN HISTORY

Plymouth Colony became part of the larger Massachusetts Bay Colony in 1691. The following year, Plymouth, which had grown to ten towns, sent representatives to the Massachusetts assembly for the first time. There had never been any real differences between the two colonies, and when they were united, people began to forget the "Old Colony."

It was not until the end of the eighteenth century that people started to be interested in the story of the Pilgrims and their colony. From 1769 onward, public leaders and clergymen were invited to Plymouth to give speeches on Forefathers' Day, the anniversary of the Pilgrims' landing on December 21, 1620. The most famous of these speeches was given in 1820 by the celebrated lawyer and politician Daniel Webster. Webster held up the Pilgrims as the founders of the American nation and way of life. He saw their religious separatism as arising out of a demand for religious tolerance. In the Pilgrims' efforts to build a new society in the New World, he saw the determination of his fellow Americans to expand their nation from the Atlantic to the Pacific.

Henry Cabot Lodge went still further when, in his Forefathers' Day address of 1920, he stated that these were "men with empires in their brains." The Pilgrims had become the Pilgrim Fathers, the true founders of America.

The new status of the Pilgrim settlers in U.S. culture was reflected in popular literature and art. People like Oliver Wendell Holmes, John Quincy Adams, Henry Wadsworth Longfellow, and James Russell Lowell wrote poems and stories in their honor. One of the most famous of these is the poem *The Landing of the Pilgrim Fathers*, which was written by an Englishwoman, Felicia Dorothea Hemans (1793–1835), and set to music by her sister, Mary Anne Brown.

The famous landing at Plymouth rock was captured in heroic paintings by Henry Sargent (*right*) as well as in engravings and woodcuts. Scenes of the landing even found their way to China, where they were copied onto porcelain plates and shipped around the world. The famous rock itself, which according to legend the Pilgrims used while disembarking, was enshrined under a portico. It is a major tourist attraction today, just as it was in the nineteenth century.

The modern national holiday of Thanksgiving owes its existence to Sarah Josepha Hale (*above*), who was the editor of the popular magazine *Godey's Lady's Book* in the years before the Civil War. She liked the idea of an annual thanksgiving celebration, and wrote letters to politicians encouraging them to create an official holiday. She hoped that such a day would bring the nation together and help to prevent the North and South from going to war with each other. It wasn't until 1863, at the height of the Civil War, that President Abraham Lincoln declared a day of thanksgiving for the Union victory at Gettysburg. The holiday stuck and came to be associated with the Pilgrims' 1621 harvest celebration. To this day the fourth Thursday of November is a time for roast turkey, pumpkin pie, family gatherings, and re-creation of the Pilgrims' first Thanksgiving.

THE PILGRIM COLONY IN TIME

J onathan Prentiss arrived in the New World in 1621 and his wife Rebecca in 1625. The Prentisses and the Winsteads are fictitious characters, but they are included below among some of the related events that actually took place in the Old World and the New World, both before and after the period of this book.

1455 Johannes Gutenberg completes publication of the Bible using his new invention, the moveable-type printing press. Before this time, books had to be copied by hand and were therefore very expensive.

1487–88 Bartolomeu Dias sails around the southern tip of Africa, opening the way for Portuguese trade with India and the Far East.

1492 Christopher Columbus makes his first voyage to the New World, setting the stage for Spanish conquests in the Caribbean, Mexico, Central America, and South America.

1497 King Henry VII of England sponsors John Cabot's voyage of exploration. Both Cabot and his son were to claim lands for the English Crown in Nova Scotia, Newfoundland, and Labrador.

1518 Beginnings of the Protestant Reformation in Germany, with the work of Martin Luther.

1534 Henry VIII's Act of Supremacy marks the beginning of the Reformation in England.

1585 Sir Walter Ralegh unsuccessfully attempts to establish an English colony on Roanoke Island, off the coast of what is now North Carolina.

1588 The English fleet defeats the Spanish Armada, which had been sent to invade England.

1597 A group of Puritans attempt to establish a colony on the Magdalen Islands off the coast of Canada. The colony fails, and the Puritans go to Holland instead.

1599 Rebecca is born in London. A year later Jonathan is born in Essex.

1606 The Separatists establish their first church in the village of Scrooby, in northern England.

1607 First permanent English colony in the New World is established at Jamestown, Virginia.

1607–8 Members of the Separatist church at Scrooby flee to Holland and become known as Pilgrims.

1608 Frenchman Samuel de Champlain establishes a trading post at Quebec. Capitalizing on the trade in furs, the French quickly follow up by establishing many other trading posts along the St. Lawrence River.

1611 William Shakespeare writes *The Tempest*, a play based on accounts of travel to Bermuda and Virginia. Bermuda is at this time known as the "Isle of Devils," and sailors are afraid to land there.

1620 The *Mayflower* brings the Pilgrims to Plymouth.

1621 Jonathan Prentiss comes to Plymouth Colony on the *Fortune*.

1625 Charles I becomes king of England and begins a series of repressive measures against the Puritans. Rebecca and her husband come to Plymouth; he dies in the winter of that year.

1626 Jonathan and Rebecca are married.

1630 About 700 Puritans from England, unhappy with the religious policies of Charles I, establish the Massachusetts Bay Colony. This begins the "Great Migration" of over 40,000 Puritans to New England.

1636 The General Court of Massachusetts approves plans to found a college at New Towne (now Cambridge). The college is later named in honor of John Harvard, a minister who left a generous bequest of books.

1638 Edward Jeffrey finishes his apprenticeship and is granted six acres of land on Cape Cod at the spring meeting of the court. The next spring, he marries a woman who has recently arrived from the Massachusetts Bay Colony and begins building a house.

1642 Civil war breaks out in England between supporters of the king and supporters of Parliament, including many Puritans. In the course of the war, the King, Charles I, is executed and a Puritan, Oliver Cromwell, comes to power as Lord Protector of England. Without anti-Puritan pressures in England, the "Great Migration" to Massachusetts ends.

1656 Rebecca buys a share in an ironworks recently established at Taunton.

1657 William Bradford, governor of Plymouth for nearly 30 years , dies.

1675 King Philip's War breaks out between colonists and Indians. Thomas Prentiss serves in the war as a captain .

1679 Isaac's son, Samuel Winstead, is admitted to Harvard College.

1691 Plymouth Colony is incorporated into the Massachusetts Bay Colony.

1697 Samuel Winstead, now a minister, records the reminiscences of his aged father, Isaac, concerning the early years of the Old Colony. He later donates a copy to the Harvard College Library.

1769 The Old Colony Club is founded in Plymouth and institutes "Forefathers' Day" on the anniversary of the Pilgrims' landing.

1820 Daniel Webster's speech on "Forefathers' Day" praises the Pilgrim colonists as the true founders of America.

1863 Abraham Lincoln proclaims Thanksgiving as a national holiday.

GLOSSARY

Adventurer Like modern investors, seventeenth-century adventurers were people who were willing to risk their money in the hope of making more money. A popular way for adventurers to invest was through a joint-stock company (*see below*) like the one that funded the Pilgrims' voyage, which permitted the adventurers to pool their money and share the risk.

Bandolier A belt with small pouches or loops to hold ammunition for guns.

Beam and Draft The beam of a ship is its width from side to side at the widest point. The draft is its depth below the water line.

Bushel A unit of volume, about 2,150 cubic inches or 35.24 liters, the size of a modern "bushel basket."

Buttery A pantry where food and drink are kept.

Colony A region that is under the political control of a distant country and has been settled by people either from that country or sponsored by that country.

Dugout A house constructed partly below and partly above ground. New arrivals in the colonies frequently built this type of house to survive the first winter.

Elder In the Pilgrim Church, the elder was the highest lay leader (that is, not an ordained minister) of the church. When the Pilgrims came to the New World, they left their minister, John Robinson, behind in Holland. Their elder, William Brewster, presided over church services and delivered sermons for many years, although he could not give communion.

Freemen Men permitted to vote in the colony.

General Court A gathering of all the freemen in the colony. The court had the authority to pass laws, impose taxes, and try crimes. It met four times a year.

Gristmill A mill that grinds grain by crushing it between rotating wheels of stone.

Hasty Pudding A porridge made by boiling flour or cornmeal in water.

Joint-Stock Company A company that made it possible to raise the money required to establish and maintain trading settlements like Plymouth Colony. Individual adventurers (investors) would put up money in the hope of claiming some of the future profits of the settlement.

Matchlock Musket The matchlock musket was more like a small cannon than a modern gun. It was fired by lighting the gunpowder directly with a small taper, which had to be lit and carried around just for that purpose. This was especially hard to do if the weather was bad!

Mayflower Compact Shortly before the Pilgrims landed at Plymouth, the adult males who were not servants signed a document called the Mayflower Compact. In signing this compact (agreement), they promised to abide by any laws that they might make as freemen (*see above*) of the colony.

Meetinghouse A large building, maintained by the colony, in which church services and meetings of the General Court were held. In the early years of the Plymouth Colony, the meetinghouse was also used as a fort.

Mortar and Pestle A mortar (shaped like a bowl) and a pestle (shaped like a stick) can be used to grind herbs and spices for medicines or cooking.

Palisade A sturdy fence made of vertical logs, intended for defense.

Pompion A Dutch name for pumpkin.

Pottle An old measure of volume, about two quarts.

Sabbath For the Pilgrims the Sabbath was Sunday, the day of the week reserved for church services, rest, and religious contemplation.

Saints and Strangers The saints were the original members of the separatist Pilgrim church in Leyden, while the strangers were ordinary English folk who accompanied them on their voyages to the New World.

Settle A long high-backed wooden bench. The high back keeps off drafts during cold winter evenings.

Smallpox A deadly disease that was very common in the seventeenth century. Those who survived the disease were usually left with pockmarks on their skin.

Tuberculosis A deadly disease chiefly affecting the lungs that was common in the seventeenth century.

Undertaker During the buyout of 1627, the undertakers were the few colonists who pledged their personal credit to buy the adventurers' (*see above*) stakes in the colony. To pay off the debt that they incurred, they used the proceeds of the fur trade.

Volley The firing of guns at the same time and in the same direction. Doing this requires lots of regular practice, coordination, and a skilled commanding officer.

Wigwam A low hut with an arched roof. The walls and roof can be made of reeds, bark, skins, or mats woven out of grass. Some settlers adopted this Indian design during their first year before they could build wooden houses.

INDEX

INDEX

Places to Visit

Pilgrim Hall Museum
75 Court Street (Route 3A)
Plymouth, MA 02360
Phone: (508) 746-1620
Fax: (508) 747-4228
www.pilgrimhall.org

Plimoth Plantation
P.O. Box 1620
Plymouth, MA 02362
Phone: (508) 746-1622
Fax: (508) 746-4978
www.plimoth.org

Salem 1630: Pioneer Village
Forest River Park
Salem, MA 01970
(978) 744-0991
www.7gables.org/1630.html

Acknowledgments

Breslich & Foss would like to thank William Carlson, Ted Hinman, Maria Jiminez, Merrill Kohlhofer, David A. Olson, Chuck Schiffendecke, Julia Stitson, Christine E. Tremblay, Keith Willis, William Walker.

Paul Erickson would like to thank the staff of Breslich & Foss, the staff of the Salem 1630: Pioneer Village, and his family.

Picture Credits
Courtesy of the Pilgrim Society, Plymouth, Massachusetts: pp. 40-41, 42-43
Plimoth Plantation, pp. 5, 6-7, 11 (top right), 25 (right), 34 (bottom)
Nigel Bradley pp. 22-23 (center), pp. 24-25 (center)
All other photographs by Miki Slingsby
All artwork by John James